WORK AND THE CITY

FRANK DUFFY

black dog publishing
london uk

THE EDGE
FUTURES

By the year 2025 the climate will have changed irrevocably, mainly as a result of greenhouse gas emissions. The temperature is predicted to be, on average, half a degree warmer and will fluctuate to a greater extent. Rainfall will have reduced but will also become more extreme. Resources such as energy, water and food imports will be in shorter supply and transport will be constrained; partly as a result of climate change but also due to regulations aimed at preventing global warming. In this series of important and timely books the Edge explore the impact these changes will have on our lives in the future. Global in scope and far reaching in its implications this series examines the significant social, environmental, political, economic and professional challenges that we face in the years ahead.

CONTENTS

FOREWORD
DAVID GANN

Frank Duffy's text extends a long stream of work that he has led in helping us to understand the forces that shape the built environment and how the industry that produces and operates it needs to embrace innovation. In particular, Duffy has enabled us to understand the relationships between people, work processes and the changing nature of place within which work is carried out.

25 years ago there was excitement about the technological possibilities offered by Information and Communication Technologies for monitoring and controlling the built environment. Liberalisation of financial services and telecommunications in the UK, with growth of digital trading and digital media, ushered in the so-called intelligent building. Companies like IBM and BT predicted new patterns of telework as the service sector grew, supported by a new digital infrastructure. Concerns were growing about the impact of business and society on the natural environment. People talked about the coming of the 'knowledge economy'. This was 15 years before the birth of the World Wide Web and massive growth of cheap air travel, which has had such profound impact on historic city infrastructures and created demand for brand new cities.

Since then, planners and developers have struggled to cope with the changing requirements of businesses and consumers, whilst controlling the damaging excesses of globalisation and rapid urbanisation on the natural environment. Those responsible for designing, managing and adapting buildings faced a dilemma—the need to make decisions about long-lived capital investments in the context of what are often much shorter-term changes in the ways in which people live and work—without adequate data and knowledge to make such decisions.

Yet the technologies that underpin this recent wave of economic growth and patterns of societal change hold part of the key to how we might better manage the fabric of our cities, their development and regeneration. It is technically possible to 'instrument' the built environment and the activities that take place within it, in a way that provides rich data and feedback about how we might use it more productively, providing vibrancy and choice for citizens, whilst controlling pollution of the natural environment.

Moreover, a combination of eScience and Grid computing linked with simulation and visualisation technologies and the internet offer a platform of tools—Innovation Technology—that can enable designers and users to work together to find better options. Exciting developments in virtual prototyping of systems and services is, for the first time, unlocking new possibilities for managing the flow of energy, water, transportation, communications and healthcare in cities. For example, Imperial College is one of the universities at the forefront of some of these developments. Its BP Urban Energy Systems Centre has devised a 'Synthetic City model enabling energy systems to be planned and balanced, working on projects such as the Dongtan eco-city in China. Similar developments can be seen in healthcare with new approaches to research using medical imaging and delivery through Polyclinics.

As Duffy reminds us, to unlock the promise of Innovation Technology for future development and management of the built environment, the multifarious range of professionals associated with its production and use will need to find new and better ways of working together. Design London—a joint venture between the Royal College of Art and Imperial's Business School and Engineering Faculty—offers a model for integrated design of market and user-facing services, engineering the systems that support them with business models that enable them to be delivered efficiently and profitably. These new research centres provide immersive simulation environments in which research and industry can collaborate in interdisciplinary teams.

Built environment professionals in the UK have a wonderful opportunity to work at the leading edge of these developments, breaking away from historic professional and industrial demarcation boundaries with the goal of integrating the design and development of the physical and digital economy.

INTRODUCTION

Work is such a large subject and has attracted such a huge literature in recent years that in examining the changing nature of the workplace I have found it necessary to concentrate on two predominant themes, first, the impact of information technology in changing conventions in the use of space and time and secondly how this impact may be related to climate change and to saving the planet.

1 Handy, Charles, *Understanding Organizations*, Harmondsworth: Penguin, 1967

2 Castells, Manuel, *The Information Age: Economy: Society: Culture*, Oxford: Blackwell, 1996

3 Davenport, Tom, *Thinking for a Living*, Harvard, CT: Harvard Business School Press, 2005

4 Sennett, Richard, *The Culture of the New Capitalism*, New Haven, CT: Yale University Press, 2006

5 Sassen, Saskia, *A Sociology of Globalization*, New York: Norton, 2006

6 Kelly, Tom, *The Art of Innovation*, Profile Business, 2002, Moggridge, Bill, *Designing Interactions*, Cambridge, MA: MIT Press, 2006

7 Dodgson, Gann and Salter, *Think, Play, Do*, Oxford, 2005

8 Mitchell, William J, *City of Bits*, Cambridge, MA: MIT Press, 1995

The discussion that follows has been enlarged and enriched by Charles Handy's interest in new forms of organisation and new kinds of career[1]; Manuel Castells' writing on the impact of informational networks on urban form[2]; Laurence Prusak and Tom Davenport on how Knowledge Management effects organisational structure[3]; Richard Sennett on the ethics of post industrial society[4]; Saskia Sassen on the sociology of the Knowledge Economy[5]; Tom Kelley and Bill Moggridge (both from the product design company, IDEO) on ways of enhancing the relationship between people and machines to stimulate innovation[6]; David Gann on innovation in the Construction Industry[7]; and, of course, Bill Mitchell on the nature of the 'City of Bits' to whom I am indebted for the leading idea that has shaped my argument.[8]

This book is necessarily retrospective as well as prospective. It is a response to an invitation to contribute to Edge Futures some views on the future of the working environment and particularly the office building in the light of accelerating climate change and of the consequent imperative to design workplaces and, indeed, entire urban structures in less wasteful and destructive ways. Obviously these are topics of very great practical importance and indeed urgency. However, after a 40 year career spent almost entirely in the world of work, I find myself unwilling to be confined at this particular moment in history to an exclusively environmental interpretation of this brief. What strikes me most forcibly today about the office as a building type is how unstable and subject to change are the emerging workplaces of the knowledge economy and how absurdly wasteful in every possible way are practically all the architectural stereotypes and delivery processes for workplaces that we have inherited from the nineteenth and twentieth centuries. Given unprecedented access to increasingly powerful information technology, which is more than capable of unleashing a tidal wave of wide ranging and fundamental societal and economic change, we need far more radical solutions than simply patching up environmental problems in existing office typologies, including making office buildings less leaky, greener and more sustainable.

To invent the future we need to escape from the past and yet paradoxically to escape from the past we have to engage with history to understand it as fully as possible. We need to deploy critical intelligence to understand why office work and the office as a building type developed in the way they did, distinguishing between features that may continue to be valid and those that appear to be rapidly becoming redundant, irrelevant and even downright dangerous. Architects in particular, if we are to be free to invent, need to know where existing office typologies came from, how they have developed and why so many features of conventional office environments are becoming inadequate, dysfunctional and divorced from emerging modes of living and working.

The changes that we are currently experiencing in the nature of work are at least as drastic, far-reaching and irreversible as the impact, two hundred years ago, of the Industrial Revolution on English society and the English landscape. The initial impetus that set in motion both the earlier and contemporary changes is technological—the harnessing of the power latent in water and steam in the late eighteenth and early nineteenth centuries and the harnessing of the power of the computer and telecommunications in our own time. The cultural, social and psychological consequences of these technological advances are far more profound than the physical transformations they have engendered.

Nevertheless the physical fabric of our buildings and cities, not least workplaces, will change: to paraphrase a famous remark on architecture by Winston Churchill, we use technology and then technology uses us. Writing from an architectural perspective, it is tempting to focus on the first of the two dimensions of technologically induced change that I propose to discuss—the ways in which the physical fabric of buildings and cities are being changed by information technology. However, equally important, if not more so, are the ways in which information technology is making it possible for us to reinvent the dimension of time by dissolving temporal conventions that have been taken for granted for centuries. Powerful, robust, reliable and ubiquitous information technology, epitomised by the BlackBerry and the iPod, will ensure that the ways in which we use both space and time will have to be completely rethought and restructured.

ARCHITECTS WHO CAN'T SAY NO

Can I and my architect colleagues really be trusted to come up with a sufficiently rigorous and all-encompassing approach to addressing the contribution that office buildings are making to climate change? Most of us architects are temperamentally, institutionally and economically biased towards doing what we like most, i.e. designing new buildings. Acculturated, as we are, within the construction industry, we are deeply imbued with the can-do, supply-side dominated culture of our trade. We are flattered when developers, whether in Dubai, London, Moscow, New York or Shanghai, ask us to design large amounts of undifferentiated office space for what they take for granted as an infinitely expanding market. But what makes us so sure that developers know what they are doing?

The architect's role has always been to operate at the hinge point between supply and demand. Our principal professional ethic, as Sir John Soane pointed out long ago, demands that we are even-handed in arbitrating between the demands of clients and the just expectations of builders.[9] However, my own observation is that we architects frequently find ourselves slipping back into a collective default position: based on the implicitly self-serving belief that new buildings, innovative buildings, more buildings, any buildings are the inevitable answer to whatever problems our clients have to address. What would we do, or rather, what should we do if science and common sense were to tell us that building too many new office buildings is to continue to create a substantial part of the environmental problem? Only recently, under the pressure of the accelerating debate around sustainability, has the idea begun to grow that perhaps not more office buildings but rather fewer buildings, more intelligently and intensively used, would be a far more sensible contribution not only to each of our clients' actual requirements but more importantly to the long-term habitability of the planet.

9 Quoted in Duffy, Francis, *Architectural Knowledge*, London: E&FN Spon, 1998

We are not alone in this crisis. The entire construction industry shares the same blind spots. One very common tendency is to focus uneven attention on the energy performance of superficial features of buildings, especially the ones that are easy to see, for example; fritted glazing, green roofs and walls, photovoltaic panels and wind mills. "That's an interesting idea for a facade" we think as we glance though the architectural magazines. But do we pay sufficient attention to the way buildings perform as a whole and particularly to how they are used over time?

The step by step, box-ticking methodologies of both BREEAM and LEED, useful as these voluntary building rating methods may sometimes be in environments unconstrained by dwindling resources, in no way encourage architects,

developers or the construction industry to abandon our
new build bias. In fact, rather the opposite is the case.
Step by step evaluative methods cannot be relied upon
to stimulate strategic insights into the environmental
specifications and physical features that matter most under
specific circumstances.

Invisible processes and patterns of use never attract
the same level of architectural attention even if they are
demonstrably efficient or inefficient. Quite simply: they do
not catch our eye.

As serial purveyors of new buildings it is hard for us to
take the longer view. Perhaps some calculations would
help. If we were to aggregate the floor areas of all office
buildings, we would find that new buildings comprise only
a relatively small subset of the total office building stock in
our cities, town centres and business parks. Mature cities
like London replace their office building stock relatively
slowly—at the rate of no more than two to three per cent
per year, turning over the entire stock every 50 years or
so. But all this realisation does is to alert us to an even
bigger problem. Because each generation of architects
concentrates on what our clients pay us to design, i.e.
completely new buildings or new facades, what is neither
new, nor designed by us or our friends and rivals, is off our
professional map.

An even bigger blind spot is that architects have little
motivation to measure and hence no vocabulary to
describe how efficiently office buildings are occupied over
time. Because our heuristic seems to be 'Never look back',
we are unable to predict the longer term consequences
in use of what we design. Yet the handful of space
planners (such as my practice DEGW, which pioneered the
technique) who do measure building occupancy report
that even over the normal, eight hours of the working

day most office buildings are lightly occupied—well over half of conventional individual workplaces are empty, even at the busiest times of day. Meeting rooms, even when pre-booked, are also, notoriously, often empty. Total occupancy of all office workplaces, combined with meeting rooms and all other social and semi-social spaces, peaks at 60 per cent and then only for relatively short periods at the busiest times of the working day. To say that office buildings are occupied at only half their capacity is a gross understatement. The actual situation is much more wasteful. The occupancy figures quoted above relate only to eight of the 24 hours and to five out of the seven days that office buildings are theoretically available for use. Apart from some call centres and relatively rare shift-based office activities, occupancy in the remaining 16 hours, exclusive of weekends, is slim and intermittent.

Under-use of the office building stock—offices used at most for half their potential for only one third of their theoretical availability every working day—combined with a crazy craving to build more and more, given conventional working practices, seemingly inevitably half empty new office buildings create the kind of statistic that, were they to do with the availability and use of warships or aircraft, would have had a wartime Prime Minister writing angry memos to his Chiefs of Staff. Where is there an equivalent sense of crisis? I look out nightly from my window in the Barbican at lights blazing out on every floor of the splendid new office buildings that surround me, at such times more or less entirely empty, apart from cleaners and a few lost souls. It is then that I wonder whether we architects, however many BREEAM or LEED certificates we can boast of, have even reached the beginning of the beginning of the phoney war against climate change.

AT THE MILL
WITH SLAVES?

Three related questions—what kind of workplaces are we likely to need in the future; how should they be designed; and how should they be used—are closely related to environmental issues.

However, these basic architectural questions cannot be addressed without understanding how the trajectory of technological change is transforming the world of work.

Fundamental changes are emerging in the design of workplaces that could very well be to our own and the planet's collective environmental advantage. Environmental issues are only one aspect of a much bigger problem—or, as the optimists among us would see it, of a much greater opportunity. Because of rapid technological advances in the world of work the end may be in sight at long last of the dominance of the industrially based culture which over the last two hundred years has done so much environmental damage in general and which has led in particular in my own field to the gross irrationality in the use of time and resources in office buildings sketched above.

The invisible cloud of electronic connectivity that now surrounds us all, wherever we may be, means that the way buildings and cities are used over time is becoming a critically important variable in environmental design. It is no longer useful to rely upon obsolescent temporal categories, such as the five day week and the eight hour day, either to categorise office work or to measure the environmental performance of buildings. Boundaries between what is work, and is not, are shifting fast. Work itself, connected by universal networks of communications, especially the growing component of knowledge work, is spilling out into ever wider and more complex spatial and temporal

Synchrony

Co-location

landscapes. To understand the physical accommodation of knowledge work, it has already become necessary for advanced organisations to map and manage networks that transcend the boundaries of office buildings to include activities and communications that take place outside the office—at home, on the road, in the restaurant or club, in the hotel room, on the train or plane. A simple device like the BlackBerry means that the 24 hour day, the seven day week dispersed over huge geographies is already an operational reality for millions of office workers. The consequence for architects, and for everyone else involved in accommodating work, is not just that the office building no longer maintains a monopoly on accommodating office work but that the office building itself, whether from a general managerial or a specific environmental point of view, has become a highly misleading unit of analysis.

William J Mitchell, the Director of the Design Laboratory at MIT, has argued that the impact of the ubiquitous, powerful, reliable information technology, that is creating such radically new dimensions of spatial and temporal connectivity, will be of at least equivalent importance in stimulating cultural, social and behavioural change as the Industrial Revolution.[10] Information Technology is dissolving the two iron laws that for two hundred years have shaped the buildings and cities in which we accommodate work, as well as all the other related activities that make up our economic lives. These outmoded laws are firstly synchrony, the necessity of working at the same time as one's fellow workers, and secondly co-location, the necessity of working in the same place with the same people. These laws are losing their power because of the new freedoms that come from being connected electronically at all times wherever we happen to be. This is an entirely new existential condition, the importance of which it is impossible to exaggerate.

10 Mitchell, *City of Bits*

Similar seismic shifts have happened before. However, it takes historical imagination to appreciate exactly what a shock being forced for the first time to obey the novel demands of synchrony and co-location must have been to farm workers in the late eighteenth and early nineteenth centuries. Agricultural labourers, including my ancestors, were driven by economic circumstances to abandon patterns of work in the fields and on the moors that had been shaped for centuries by the slowly changing rhythms of the seasons and Saints' Days. The work pattern of the Industrial Revolution was driven by a new rhythm, the unforgiving drum beat of the machine, and by a new timetable demanding simultaneity. Working together in the mill and at the loom, controlled by the clock, the bell, the hooter and the siren, eventually became the normal pattern of life for hundreds of millions. Hence the social geography of the mill town and rows of back-to-backs and later, in the somewhat less overtly brutal but equally coercive forms of the suburb, the downtown office, the commuter train and the car park.

Even more imagination will be required to envision what the new world of universal connectivity will be like. However, one thing is certain: new temporal and social conventions must be invented that will be strong enough to take advantage of the enormous potential freedoms offered by the new technology as well as equally capable of avoiding the destructive effects of the hugely invasive power of information technology. Speaking pessimistically, the consequences could be far worse than any of the rigidities experienced in the nineteenth and twentieth centuries. Speaking optimistically; and while I doubt whether human nature is perfectible I prefer nevertheless to be optimistic; the consequences could be infinitely benign for the ways in which each one of us could choose to live and collectively for the environments and cities which we could create, inhabit and enjoy.

The major potential advantages for knowledge workers of the new technology are:

- More choices in life and work styles at every stage in an individual's career
- More individual control and greater responsibility in the use of space and time
- More stimulus, creativity and opportunities
- More interesting things to do—the social and intellectual benefits of knowledge work
- More connectivity, discourse and respect for others
- More open-endedness and richer opportunities in the ways we live our lives
- Greater capacity for, and understanding of, the need for change.

Given greater individual responsibility, major environmental advantages ought to follow. The potential advantages of distributed work for the majority perhaps of the working population include softening the impact of commuting—e.g. more home working or perhaps, more accurately, the dispersal and opening up of work regimes, leading to less intense and more irregular patterns of commuting which have the potential to eliminate time-wasting peaks in public transportation and related congestion on crowded motorways and other roads. The increasing use of tele-presence and other similar devices—which are becoming closer and closer in quality to real face to face meetings—could also substantially reduce the demand for long distance travel.

The environmental consequences are the emerging potential for:

- Reduction in overall requirements for office space
- More rational use of all kinds of space over time

- More mixed-use buildings and therefore more opportunities for intensive and interconnected use of spatial resources
- Uses that are 'mixable', i.e. capable of being easily changed over time
- Less homogenous, more differentiated and interactive space within and between buildings
- Space of different types and rental levels juxtaposed in complementary ways
- The rediscovery of how to drive harder the intellectual potential of cities, given that the city itself is such a powerful networking and communications device
- The rediscovery of serendipity—the creation of the overlapping and interstitial spaces that are immensely inherently valuable in the more loosely programmed knowledge economy.

A SOCIOLOGICAL CRITIQUE OF THE MODERN MOVEMENT

Siegfried Giedion's great theme in *Mechanisation Takes Command* is that the industrial logic of Taylorism or "Scientific Management", as it used to be called, is closely allied to the values and aspirations of the Modern Movement in architecture. Architecture, like management, is never independent of politics.[11]

The more architecture and management are presented as rational, value free and inevitable, the more dangerous are the probable social and political consequences.

11 Giedion, Siegfried, *Mechanisation Takes Command*, Oxford: Oxford University Press, 1948

Richard Sennett, the sociologist, has brought this argument up to date. He accuses Modern Movement architecture and urban design of three addictive vices:

- Addiction to the large scale. Buildings, particularly office buildings, have tended to become bigger and cruder over the twentieth century.

- Addiction to over-determined, over prescriptive building forms. Sennett uses the term 'brittle' to describe the consequent fragility and vulnerability of mono-functional buildings, including, of course, many office buildings, which are unlikely to be able to accommodate change.

- Addiction to centripetal patterns of urban development; the planners of which seem to be obsessed by concentrating on 'centres'; leading to the gross neglect of interstitial and peripheral spaces and to the erosion of the public realm.

The consequence of these tendencies is well illustrated by an exercise I conducted in 2007 with a class of Masters students from the Design School at Kingston University. Part of the intention of the exercise was to familiarise the students—most of whom were from abroad—with London since they knew little of the function, texture and meaning of the various parts of the city. From my perspective the more important part of the exercise was to compare the utility, the value and the meaning of contrasting urban forms. Consequently the students were asked to explore and report their impressions of Canary Wharf and Soho; two similarly sized chunks of London's urban fabric, each very different in physical character and in patterns of use. Canary Wharf and Soho are both economically vigorous, having attracted very different sectors in different ways. Canary Wharf accommodates large banks and closely connected financial service organisations, including some of the biggest law and accountancy practices. Soho has been successful in attracting the film industry in the form of a wide range of post-production houses, as well as fashion businesses, tourism and many forms of entertainment.

Canary Wharf

Soho

Soho's physical fabric is a low-rise but still relatively dense eighteenth century domestic pattern of narrow streets and squares overlaid by many nineteenth and twentieth century interventions and additions, including retailing and a large amount of warehouse and semi industrial space, much of which has been extensively converted to accommodate post-industrial uses. Canary Wharf, unlike Soho, has been created almost instantaneously within the last two decades on a narrow strip of land between two redundant docks. Canary Wharf is new, largely mono-functional and is dramatically cut off from the surrounding area. In urban terms the Wharf's model is the not unlike the downtown of a moderately successful, mid-sized North American city but more concentrated and without a hinterland.

Canary Wharf
Security

I asked the students to decide which of these two very different models of urban fabric would stand a better chance of remaining in beneficial use in the year 2030. Richard Sennett's criterion of not being 'brittle', i.e. having the capacity to accommodate diversity and continuing change, is particularly relevant here. The images selected by the students to illustrate their comparisons included, in the case of Soho, one astonishingly densely populated restaurant map of the area—there can be no better image of controlled permeability than a thousand highly varied and infinitely welcoming restaurant and cafe doors. On the other hand, many of the images used by the students to describe Canary Wharf emphasised techniques of exclusion—by guards and gates, by cameras and cops. From the students' perspective, the high levels of security characteristic of Canary Wharf killed permeability. Stringent security may be inevitable in post 9/11, early twenty-first century urbanism. Nevertheless Canary Wharf's manifestations of security were not easy for my students to condone—overt, controlling, spilling out into the streets, contaminating the public realm.

Combining accessibility with security is not new in urbanism. The same challenge has been tackled before, both urbanistically and architecturally, in more inventive and civilised ways. For example,

since the London of the 1820s was a chronically violent and unsafe place, Sir John Soane's new building for the Bank of England was designed to be a fortress, with pickets of armed guards and without any windows at all in its famously impregnable facade.[12] However, once within, the bank's plan opened up into a series of highly interconnected top-lit courts and banking halls, each used for a different aspect of the bank's business—courts leading onto courts, a city within a city. Within the outer curtain of external security and given protocols and rules to facilitate access for those who had the right and the need to enter, a large part of the interior of the bank was designed to be accessible not only to the financial services industry of the day but was also made available to a wider and, of course, privileged section of the public, including, as actually happened, tourists looking for amusement, interest and stimulation. Meanwhile, underneath their feet, in the vaults, under conditions of the highest security, lay the nation's reserve of gold. What the memory of Soane's extraordinary building demonstrates is that it is possible to take security into account and yet simultaneously achieve, through designing a series of attractive, accessible and even popular places, great architecture and great urbanism.

The Bank of England

12 Abramson, Daniel M, *Building the Bank of England*, New Haven, CT: Yale University Press, 2005

To invent appropriate forms for the cities and buildings
of the twenty-first century and to create open but secure
environments for the enterprises that will be increasingly
characteristic of the complex, fluid and interactive knowledge
economy, we will need to reverse the unfortunate way,
accurately diagnosed by Richard Sennett, in which cities and
buildings have been shaped by the habits and presumptions
of the industrial era.[13]

13 Talk give by
Richard Sennett
at the Urban Age
Conference in
Mumbai, 2007

How can cities be designed to provide close adjacencies
between different scales of workplace and many
complementary functions? How can we create matrices of
stimulating and attractive places where the probability of
interaction of all kinds, social, intellectual, commercial, is
stimulated, perhaps to the margins of inevitability? It is striking
that the three world cities in which such conditions still exist
to a large extent; London, New York and Paris; are cities
which are densely developed, share the benefits of a mix of
grandeur and ordinariness, are endowed with a high degree
of physical complexity and whose long histories of growth and
development antedate the Modern Movement.

REDESIGNING THE SUPPLY CHAIN

A possibly more fruitful and less nostalgic line of enquiry may be to investigate the underlying economic reasons why the inherent advantages of these three great and highly successful cities are being threatened by large scale, segregated, predominantly office developments such as Canary Wharf, the emerging World Trade Center and La Defense. These projects illustrate very clearly the architectural consequences of particular sequences of funding, designing and delivering office buildings and demonstrate how urgent it is that the powerful 'supply chain' that shaped them is challenged and opened up to critical enquiry.

The office supply chain that I am questioning has been dominant for well over a century in the United States, the United Kingdom and other countries strongly influenced by Anglo-American real estate practice. The chain operates at three levels: the first is the financing and development of office buildings, the second, the designing and delivery of such buildings, and the third is the way in which corporate real estate acquires and facilities managers run office buildings for the alleged benefit of users. The chain begins with money looking for a home. It moves from developers getting their hands on this money to the processes involved in design and construction and culminates in eventual occupation by end users. It is taken for granted that it is in everyone's interest on the supply side of the office development and construction industries to make projects happen whatever the environmental, social or business cost.

The principal actors and major responsibilities within the conventional Anglo-American office supply chain are:

- Finance and Development: from Investors to Developers, Lawyers, Letting Agents and Real Estate Brokers—the parties who determine the financial and market feasibility of a project;

- Design and Construction: from the Architect via the Planners to the Cost Consultants, various kinds of Engineer, Project Managers, to the Construction Industry and its Sub-Contractors and Suppliers—the parties who determine the practical feasibility of a project;

- Corporate Real Estate and Facilities Management: from Corporate Real Estate to Facilities Managers via Human Resources and Information Technology to Department Heads and to End Users—the parties who take possession of a project.

Four remarkable features distinguish the office development supply chain from other somewhat more sophisticated supply chains—such as retailing, a business sector which, despite many manifest weaknesses and much squandering of resources, at least measures footfall systematically and is able to react whenever design resources are not being used to maximum effect—within this industry's own terms, of course. In contrast office development as a business sector:

- likes to operate independently of other building types and uses;

- moves remorselessly forward, always in the same direction;

- is almost impossible to stop once set in motion—since interruptions generate great costs and inconvenience for everyone involved;

- has small appetite for absorbing and responding to feedback of any kind, at any time, between any of the levels or any of the parties involved.

Of the four the last feature is the most surprising. But perhaps one should not be surprised that such a markedly supply-side orientated system is very bad at learning from experience.

There are circumstances in which a strong supply-side bias may be tolerably safe and even convenient—for example, given a stable economic environment, relatively little technological innovation and a predictable relationship between supply and demand. However, in the context of today's rapid technological and social change, failure to learn from and respond to emerging circumstances is certain to lead to trouble. Taking invisible processes for granted and without question in a time of change seems to me to have great potential for generating highly visible urban disasters—

not least by increasing the probability of failure to respond to the challenges of environmental sustainability.

Architects who have been brought up within the Anglo-American office development process, which has been so successful throughout the entire twentieth century to the extent of being perhaps the largest and most visible influence on urban form world-wide, are particularly vulnerable if we are tempted to regard the office supply chain as definitive, inevitable, unquestionable. Such complacent passivity could very well be a huge mistake. The important point is that supply chain that I have described above is neither God given nor pre-ordained. It is a cultural artefact, a series of conventions that have grown up in particular economic, political and social circumstances. When circumstances change conventions such as these can, and indeed, must be challenged. Something better may be conceivable.

HOW THE OFFICE DEVELOPED

Where did the offices that we know so well—and the supply chain that created them—come from?

The cultural origins of the Anglo-American office supply chain are intimately connected with the work of the same Frederick Taylor, mentioned above in connection with Giedion's investigations of the origins of Modernism.

Taylor's invention of "Scientific Management" is widely and correctly recognised as having had a profound impact on many aspects of twentieth century life.[14] What is less well-known is that a very different kind of office building (emerging from a very different set of values and delivered by a very different supply chain) developed in Northern Europe as a result of a post-Second World War rejection of the application of Taylorist principles to office work.

14 Taylor, Frederick, *The Principles of Scientific Management*, New York: Harper & Brothers, 1911

This reaction was facilitated by a very different allocation of responsibilities for financing, designing and managing office buildings and has resulted, very visibly, in a highly innovative, alternative form of office architecture.

The history of these two quite different lines of development of office building types demonstrates that alternative ways of developing office buildings can and indeed do exist. Different office ideologies have led to different office architectures. Alternative supply chains have been established that have been appropriate in different circumstances. Such differences have not been arbitrary but relate to varying economic, technological, cultural and political circumstances. Pointing out that such differences have existed in the past is an essential step in this argument. The acknowledgement that such differences exist legitimises, in the context of massive technological change and in an even bigger environmental crisis, the search for the new types of office buildings and the invention of new models of supply chain better able to accommodate the emerging requirements of the twenty-irst century knowledge economy.

15 Taylor, *The Principles*

Frederick Taylor's ideas about Scientific Management were revolutionary in their day.[15] They were phenomenally successful because Taylor discovered in a rapidly growing economy, hungry for labour, that great efficiencies in industrial production could be achieved by disregarding skilled crafts protected by centuries of guild training and by redesigning work from first principles. Workmen, who were regarded as units of production, were instructed to do exactly as they were told by experts in white overalls with stopwatches and clip boards. As manager of a production line the last thing you wanted was to allow silver haired craftsmen—who were anyway in chronically short supply in North America—any discretion in the way they carried out their work. To maximise efficiency work had to be directed by superior knowledge from above. Control and organisation became far more important than individual intelligence. Discipline and obedience in following the formula were vital.

The Seagram Building, Mies van der Rohe, 1958

Henry Ford learned everything from Frederick Taylor. It may also be worth mentioning that Hitler and Stalin were also among Frederick Taylor's greatest fans.

These technical and managerial ideas played a hugely important part in creating the wealth of the US in the twentieth century. An important by-product of Taylorism was the application of his techniques by Frank Gilbreth and others to office work—at first relatively tiny, almost insignificant component of the total workforce.[16] This shift happened most visibly in Chicago, where the high-rise office building was invented on the basis not just of the steel frame, the elevator and the curtain wall (as architectural histories record) but because of two other, arguably more influential, kinds of innovation—in real estate practice and the parallel mechanisation of office work. The combination of these inventions produced the largely developer-led, North American, high-rise office which throughout the twentieth century had such a visible impact on the skylines of cities all over the world.

The iconography of the Taylorist office reflects, as one would expect, the imposition of an overarching, standardising order—internally in ceiling grids, externally in cladding. The North American office reached a magnificent architectural apogee in the 1960s in cities such as New York, Chicago and San Francisco—splendid examples of the use of external architecture to express commercial, and ultimately political ideals. The subsequent relative decline of the North American office has been more evident internally rather than externally. Interior features which emerged in the 1970s include the universal 'cube' workstation. The cube, much mocked by the cartoonist Scott Adams, should be taken seriously both as a symptom and as a symbol of bureaucratic breakdown. Remorselessly regular layouts, within very deep offices, which provide neither privacy nor cohesion cannot be interpreted as the provision of equal benefits. The cube

16 Gilbreth, FB, *Motion Study*, New York: Van Nostrand, 1911

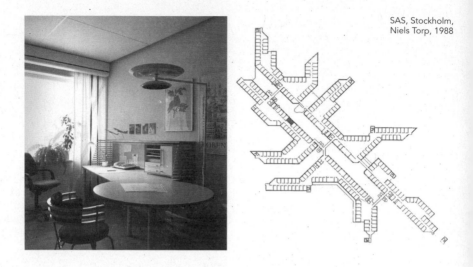

SAS, Stockholm,
Niels Torp, 1988

represents an equal distribution of misery within which
anyone and everyone can be replaced in any order and at
any time—the essentially heartless utilitarian and eventually
militaristic vision, that lies at the heart of and is the principal
strength and weakness of Taylorism.

That a strong reaction against the Taylorist office occurred in
post-Second World War Northern Europe is evidence of how
rapidly an essentially political idea can lead to the adoption
of alternative managerial practices and different forms of
architectural expression.[17]

17 Duffy, Francis,
*The Changing
Workplace*,
London: Phaidon,
1992

In the 1960s and early 1970s, in an economically resurgent
Northern Europe, a novel form of office building was
invented which was deliberately intended to be an expression
of democratic egalitarianism. The new type of office was
primarily a means of protecting the rights of each individual
office worker. Democratically elected Workers' Councils
played an important part in creating the demand for this
novel form of working environment. The objective of these

highly cellular European offices was neither efficiency nor the easy relocation of staff but the provision of excellent working conditions for all. In democratic societies, disturbed and shaken by memories of Fascism, it became axiomatic that all office workers should have an equal right to every possible individual environmental benefit; fresh air and sunlight, quiet and privacy.

The architectural consequence is an office type widespread in Germany, Scandinavia and The Netherlands which I have called the "Social Democratic" office in order to distinguish it from the North American Taylorist office. A classic example of such a Social Democratic office is Niels Torp's SAS headquarters in Stockholm.[18] This is an office building shaped as a series of pavilions which together accommodate hundreds of individual rooms, all naturally lit and ventilated, all the same size, each with an individually controllable environment and each equipped with tasteful and ergonomic furniture and sound proof partitions. The message self-consciously projected by the architecture of this building is that SAS is a modern, equal opportunity, democratic organisation which dislikes the display of hierarchy and wishes to encourage employees to make their own decisions about how and when to get their work done. The 'street' which is the main collective feature of the interior of the building—as well as yet another symbol of the organisation's values—is top-lit, lined by restaurants, cafes and other amenities, beautifully planted, and leads to an entrancing exterior view of a lake set in parkland. The glass boardroom, projected above the street, broadcasts a similar message: transparency, accessibility and accountability.

18 Duffy, Francis, *The New Office*, London: Conran Octopus, 1997

What is less obvious is that an entirely different delivery process had been necessary to create the Social Democratic office, a type of building that would be unlikely to be conceived and, even more fundamentally, almost impossible to finance,

construct, deliver or justify within a Taylorist work culture.
The layers of responsibility and the principal actors within
the supply chain for the Social Democratic office are:

- Finance and Development: provided and managed by
  business owners themselves who are frequently private
  owners, and in some cases members of the same
  family, who will tend to judge the financial feasibility of
  a new building primarily on a longer term operational
  basis rather than as an investment the value of which is
  expected to be released quickly by exchange or sale.
  Insiders determine the utility, value and meaning of
  the project not the external real estate market;

- Design and Construction: from an Architect chosen
  by the user-client through open competition who
  is allowed to assemble his or her own handpicked
  team of Cost Consultants and various kinds of
  Engineer, through a Planning System, tending to
  be deferential to the architect, onwards to the
  Construction Industry and to sub-contractors and
  Suppliers again forming a more cohesive team than
  is usual in the Anglo Saxon world. In this system the
  parties who determine the quality of the product
  and deliver it are likely to be more coherent and less
  confrontational.

- Corporate Real Estate and Facilities Management:
  from Corporate Real Estate to Facilities Managers
  via Human Resources and Information Technology
  to Department Heads to End Users, all of whom
  are likely to be directly involved in maintaining the
  success of the client's business. These parties are
  likely to view their building not just as yet another
  office building but as an instrument specifically
  designed to ensure the success of their own
  particular business.

Who is to say that this supply chain isn't more productive in economic terms than the Taylorist model? The most important lesson to be derived from the Social Democratic model of the office is not that it is necessarily superior to the Taylorist model, although in some ways it obviously is, but that the history of the development of this model and indeed its very existence demonstrate that alternative types of office building and alternative delivery processes become legitimate as circumstances and values change.

HOW BUILDINGS LEARN

New thinking about the nature of office buildings and about how they should be delivered is necessary at a time such as the present, when there is great likelihood of change.

Office buildings and time are highly correlated. When I was a masters student in the School of Architecture at Berkeley in 1967–1968, one of the most admired professors was Christopher Alexander, who had recently invented what he called "the Pattern Language", a design based on assembling essential design propositions, each capturing a balance of social or environmental forces.

Some of Alexander's patterns are small-scale and domestic, others reach out to address urban issues. Once a pattern is articulated, it is in the public realm and can be replicated and related to other patterns to assemble environments cumulatively which are increasingly free of the blunders and contradictions that disfigure so many of our buildings and cities.

Alexander's title for the first book in his series promoting the Pattern Language is *The Timeless Way of Building*.[19] I learned many things from Christopher Alexander but perhaps the most important is negative: buildings are anything but timeless. They are, in fact, very much the opposite: not so much built out of eternal bronze and marble, nor even concrete, steel and glass but out of a whole series of layers of materials with varying degrees of longevity. Some elements of buildings are long lasting, capable of persisting potentially for centuries. Others are designed to respond to corporate clients' medium-term requirements. Yet other elements are intended to satisfy individual users' sometimes very short-term needs.[20]

19 Alexander, Christopher, *The Timeless Way of Building*, Oxford: Oxford University Press, 1979

20 Duffy, Cave, Worthington, *Planning Office Space*, London: The Architectural Press, 1976

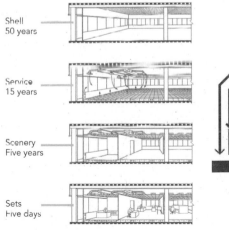

Shell
50 years

Service
15 years

Scenery
Five years

Sets
Five days

Shell, Services, Scenery, Sets.

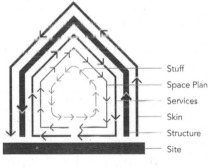

Stuff
Space Plan
Services
Skin
Structure
Site

Site, Structure, Services, Scenery, Sets, Stuff

This point of view is well expressed by Stewart Brand in his book, *How Buildings Learn*.[21] Brand is fascinated by what happens to buildings after they are built and is interested in what makes it possible for both buildings and cities to mature and develop. "Structures persist", "interiors are flighty", "buildings tell stories", are three key phrases from his book. The most successful buildings and cities, according to Brand, are those that have the capacity to accommodate multiple interventions by users over the years, decades and centuries in a welcoming and graceful way.

21 Brand, Stewart, *How Buildings Learn*, New York: Viking Press, 1994

I had learned the practical essentials of what became Brand's theme somewhat earlier, in New York, in the late 1960s when I first came into contact with space planning practice, an area of professional design activity that was little-known and less understood in Europe at the time. Space planning is based on a sharp and highly practical division between design responsibilities related directly to the longevity of the things designed.

This system, also invented within the early twentieth century explosion of invention in American real estate and construction practice described above, is in itself a very Tayloristic, divide and rule, concept. Architects, working for developers, design office building shells, i.e. foundations, roof, structure and skin; anticipating a life expectancy of several decades, let us say 50 years. Service engineers, also working for developers, design air conditioning, elevators and other major items of building services to fit within the shell, anticipating a life expectancy of only 15 or so years, because of the more transitory nature and more rapid obsolescence of mechanical equipment. Space planners and interior designers work not for the developer but instead for the corporate clients who are to become the tenants of the developer, tenants whose time horizon is business related and consequently relatively short-term. Such tenants rarely expect to occupy the space that is fitted out for them for longer than a decade. Their actual duration of occupancy is often much shorter. This is the layer of longevity that I have called 'scenery', because of its resemblance to the ever changing apparatus we associate with the stage. The elements of scenery of 'fit out' as it is usually called—partitions, floor finishes, reception areas and furniture layouts—have a life expectancy of perhaps five to seven years depending partly upon the materiality of their products but more substantially and ultimately financially upon the terms of the leases of corporate clients. Within the premises occupied by tenant businesses, there are other layers of even more rapid transition. On a day-by-day, week-by-week, month-by-month basis, facilities managers and the office workers themselves constantly shift and rearrange the scenery as their business requirements change.

"Shell, services, scenery and sets" is a way of distinguishing between these different degrees of longevity. This concept, which I helped to introduce into a sceptical Europe in the early 1970s, which is so practical and yet in many ways so elegant, has structured my professional life ever since. It is as classic an example of American, labour-saving ingenuity as the examples that so impressed Giedion, such as the balloon frame and the

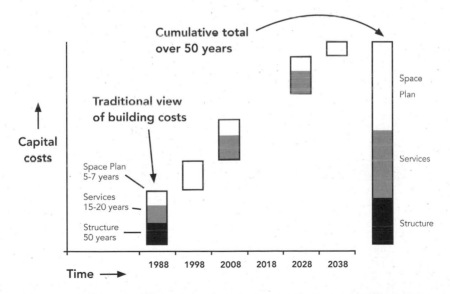

Expenditure on an office building over its lifetime i.e. architecture is a branch of interior design

production line. The idea is simple, and impersonal. It works, like the 'cube' discussed above, because the system assumes minimum communication between and maximum labour-saving among all the parties involved. It does not depend upon people knowing, understanding and liking each other: the division between the axes of architect/developer and space planner/ corporate client is notorious for generating mutual suspicion and scorn. And yet the Taylorist Office has survived for over 100 years.

Centraal Beheer, Herman Hertzberger,1972

Professional rivalry is exacerbated by economic factors. The amount of money spent once and for all on the long-term office building shell is generally far less than the sum spent cumulatively on scenery, perhaps five or six times in the normal life of an office building. "Hacks" is how I remember the architect, Philip Johnson, characterising space planners. Some interior designers argue that office architecture is simply a framework on which multiple layers of interior design can be hung, making architecture, financially speaking at any rate, a branch of interior design. Not many architects agree with this.

As I was trying to articulate the virtues of this American system for a European audience in the early 1970s I came across a rare but beautiful European example of a similar but more ideological approach to exploiting for architectural purposes the contrast between the semi-eternal nature of primary architectural forms and individual control over the short-term elements of the office interior. This was Herman Hertzberger's Centraal Beheer office building in Apeldoorn—a low-rise office building designed like an Italian village: strong and powerful, inside and out, full of voids and streets, a Platonic, pure, quasi-eternal view of architectural form.[22] Within this architectural shell the client, encouraged by Hertzberger, permitted the users to make themselves literally at home, bringing into the office their own self-selected furniture, posters and decorations, plants and even pets.

22 Duffy, Francis, *The Changing Workplace*, London: Phaidon, 1992, pp. 104–113

The architect's idea was that the users had the right to appropriate their workplaces. The frisson between long term architecture and personal choice was the idea that Hertzberger exploited formally in a very beautiful way. The reason that his notion was never replicated was because it was quickly overtaken by the parallel emergence of the much more cellular, and hence much more popular, Social Democratic office.

Totally contrasting in terms of ideas, even if it is in some ways formally similar to Centraal Beheer, is one of the most iconic—in every sense—office buildings of the early twentieth century, Frank Lloyd Wright's long demolished Larkin Building in Buffalo, New York, the relatively small, administrative centre from which the Larkin organisation's vast, surrounding array of factories and warehouses was controlled. This interior, used by Galloway as the frontispiece to his Taylorist textbook on office management, is a perfect image of a culture of control.[23] White bloused women 'typewriters' sit between black coated male clerks on steel desks purpose designed by Lloyd Wright himself of which the chief feature was that the swivel seats were cantilevered from the desk. Everyone who worked in that office had their degrees of freedom literally and figuratively controlled. The great architect himself, who thought he was a free spirit, was, as Jack Quinan has documented, very much under the control of the Larkin brothers, his clients, also geniuses, who did not hesitate to exploit Wright's talent remorselessly to express their own version of modernity.[24]

23 Galloway, L, *Office Management: Its Principles and Practice*, Oxford: The Ronald Press, 1918

24 Quinan, Jack, *Frank Lloyd Wright's Larkin Building*, Cambridge, MA: MIT Press, 1987

NEW TEMPORAL AND
SPATIAL CONVENTIONS

What new temporal and spatial conventions will be appropriate for a networked society in which ubiquitous, powerful and reliable information technology is rapidly eroding the outmoded spatial and temporal conventions of the nineteenth and twentieth centuries?

Today the nine to five timetable is becoming almost as anachronistic as the Angelus bell. Increasing mobility means that the office is no longer a stable entity in terms of place—office work can be carried out anywhere. Universal connectivity means that work is no longer constrained by temporal conventions since any connection can be made anywhere by anyone at any time.

New geographies, kinds of places and timetables are being negotiated by people who move from place to place both within and outside the conventional office. Such a high degree of mobility means that few constraints remain to determine when work ends and when the rest of life, including family and social interactions as well as leisure and intellectual and physical stimuli, begins.

Within these new dimensions of potential freedom knowledge workers can change their life styles—beneficially in many cases by making possible in different degrees a more civilised and fulfilling balance between where and when they live and work. It is arguable that many women have already benefited more than men. However, there is a dark side to this picture. Many people of both sexes are still conspicuously unsuccessful in finding a satisfying balance between work and life. In fact, is "balance" really the best word to describe the consequences of the invasion of private lives by devices such as the BlackBerry which buzzes away on the desk, at the kitchen table and by the bedside, generously delivering the 24/7 accessibility which technology has made possible? Perhaps slavery would be a closer descriptor of this new condition. What is clear is that one of the biggest challenges of the twenty-first century—even more crucial than the redesign of spatial conventions, important and closely related as time and space certainly are—is the development of new conventions in the use of time that would allow people to protect themselves from exploitation and to take advantage of the theoretical benefits that technology offers.

Redesigning the use of time implies the redesign of the physical realm. To rethink the workplace we need a much better idea of what temporal freedom and increasing mobility will mean not just within office buildings but everywhere else in the increasingly fluid and all encompassing world of work.

For example, over the last decade methods of mapping mobility in the workplace have been developed. As pointed out earlier, these demonstrate that the proportion of the working day spent by office workers within office buildings at their own individual workstations peaks at 40 per cent. This proportion is probably declining, although the task of conducting a longitudinal analysis of data collected over this decade remains to be attempted. There is another obvious weakness in this method of data collection within the context of the wider argument being developed in this book. It is relatively easy for observers, equipped with hand held devices and following predetermined routes though office floors, to record hour by hour, over the conventional period of ten working days, whether or not office workers are in the workplace and, if so, whether they are at their desks.

However, it is much more difficult to measure what office workers are doing when they are mobile and off site. Self-reporting is unlikely to provide an accurate answer: it has been found that respondents, when asked to estimate how much time they spend at their workplaces, give very consistent but highly inaccurate replies. Actual workplace occupancy is half what people report.

Another technique, which has ironic overtones for me—a convert from Taylorism still in love with measurement—is to record the growth of the proportion of internal office space that is given over not to individual workplaces but to collective activities—particularly meeting rooms, meeting spaces, social hubs and gathering points of increasing diversity. Over my working life time the proportion of collective as opposed to individual space has risen from less than ten per cent to as much as 40 per cent and in some cases even more. Again these data are tantalisingly incomplete because in their present form they cannot cover what I suspect may be an even greater rise in the use of semi-public venues (such as Starbucks) for impromptu, off site, frequently inter-organisational meetings nor for the frequent use of off site hotels and conference centres for training and other similar events.

What these data, incomplete as they are, do clearly show is that, as the knowledge economy develops, work is becoming more plural, more social and less confined within conventional organisational boundaries. Knowledge work, almost by definition, will focus more and more on communicating, sharing and developing ideas; which are inherently communal activities, impossible for solitary individuals to perform. Meanwhile, old fashioned, individual office work consisting of elementary, repetitive tasks is being remorselessly automated. Solitary, concentrated, intellectual tasks can be carried out in many other places besides the office.

The big, open-ended question is, "Why should empowered and self-reliant people, equipped with increasingly powerful information technology, ever come to work at all?" A large part of the answer is obviously to communicate with their fellow workers and, no doubt, also to enjoy their company. All of which explains the banal observation frequently made that many contemporary office interiors are beginning to look more and more like coffee bars.

A new vocabulary is emerging to describe the widening range of mobile work experiences and work styles— "anchors and residents", "drop in centres", "virtual working", "concentrated" versus "collaborative" work. Office workers, equipped with increasingly powerful technology are making their own decisions about when and where to work. A map of the spatial configuration of many businesses has become a global network of interactions. Core physical space is diminishing while interactions that transcend and spill beyond the walls of office buildings are multiplying. As communications and mobility within and between offices increase, managing such universes of interconnectivity has become a major corporate responsibility.

And yet paradoxically, despite increasing corporate dispersion, cities persist and are becoming bigger, busier and more crowded every year. One way of explaining this apparently contradictory phenomenon is that city life is also becoming increasingly networked—perhaps even more intensely but at a much more local scale. Virtuality seems to be complementary to physicality. The most successful and congenial cities are the ones that have the greatest density of overlapping social networks, some physical, others electronic.

It is the extent of leakage between such networks that creates serendipity, Horace Walpolt's neologism for taking advantage of unplanned but not totally unpredicted and certainly not undesired social and business encounters. Dense, overlapping, local social networks are a phenomenon of the knowledge economy that, like a kind of interactive compost seems to generate social energy and makes cities such interesting and useful places to inhabit.

MOBILITY AND PERMEABILITY

Mobile working, although vastly enhanced by information technology, is not entirely new. If you don't believe this, read Pepys' diary.

Pepys as a young servant of the Crown was always on the move—leaving his house near the Tower to go to his office next door (he was nearly but not quite a home worker);visiting his uncle in the country; down the river by wherry to supervise victualling at the Naval Yards at Deptford; by carriage down the Strand to wait on his superiors and to be accessible to the Duke of York in the court of the Palace of Westminster; then to the tavern to make music on his way home; moving about the narrow London streets, singing here, drinking there, talking everywhere.[25]

25 Trease, Geoffrey, *Samuel Pepys and his World*, London: Thames and Hudson, 1972

Pepys enjoyed a complex, highly mobile lifestyle, within the tiny London of his time. A little later, in Swift's and Addison's time, the early coffee houses signal the importance for somewhere warm and relatively neutral to be seen, to meet, to sit and to talk. Later still, in the early nineteenth century, the upper bourgeoisie invented the club—neutral ground and furnished like a palace—which was specially designed to encourage hobnobbing with professional colleagues and social acquaintances. The club offered every comfort and convenience that the aristocracy had taken for granted for centuries, except better run, all for an infinitesimal fraction of the price that lords and ladies had to pay for real palaces—a brilliant way to maximise scarce resources while encouraging intellectual and social interaction in the most enjoyable way possible.

There are alternative ways of carrying out work over space and time than sitting at the equivalent of Bob Cratchett's desk in Mr Scrooge's counting house.

There exists today, for the first time, as my DEGW colleague, Andrew Harrison, often points out, a rough equivalence in problem solving and communicative capacity between the virtual and the physical worlds.

Territoriality, stability, visibility, tangibility are the advantages of the physical realm as opposed to invisibility, networking, mobility, intangibility, which are the principal virtues of the virtual world. Many features of the virtual world are improving so rapidly that they rival and potentially outshine the characteristics of the ordinary physical world. The balance f convenience between the two worlds is shifting—probably more in the favour of the virtual than the physical. However, the degrees of permeability of both realms are comparable.

In the virtual world the accessibility of internet sites is greater than private knowledge systems. In the physical world encounters in the street are different from knowledge communities such as

← Virtual		Physical →
Knowledge systems e.g. VPN, corporate intranet	**Private** - Protected access - Individual or collaborative workspaces	e.g. head office, serviced offices, incubator spaces, home working
Extranet sites Knowledge communities e.g. collaborative, virtual environments, project extranet, video conferences	**Semi permeable** - Invited access - Collaborative project and meeting spaces	e.g. clubs, airpost lounges, institutes, schools
Internet sites e.g. information sources, chat rooms	**Public** - Open access - Informal interaction and open workspaces	e.g. cafes, hotel lobbies, the street, the city

clubs, which can only be entered under restricted conditions. The parallels between the public, the semi-permeable and the private geographies of the physical and the virtual worlds are very close.

New protocols are being created for the use of space and time which enhance the possibilities of different levels of interaction. Freedom of discourse on the internet is the reverse of the Taylorist emphasis on divide and rule.

Increasing permeability in the physical world is certain to erode the ruthless and inhuman Taylorist separation of functions that has led, as Richard Sennett has pointed out, to the neglect of interstitial spaces and to the cumulative decay of the public realm.

A critical cause of this neglect has been an under-estimation of the importance of opening up controlled degrees of accessibility which in the physical realm are essential to creating good buildings and cities and in the virtual realm are equally important in building a vibrant knowledge economy.

However, business protocols and inspired design on their own are not enough to create the places and the cities of the knowledge economy. Our cities, particularly in the Anglo-American world have been shaped by modernist values which were strongly influenced by Taylor. We need to reverse the malign aspects of the office supply chain that we have inherited from Taylorism. To achieve a sustainable environment for the knowledge economy we need to invent a new supply chain on new user friendly principles.

In fact, so different should this new supply chain be that it might be better described, using the late Steven Groak's term, as the exact opposite, a "demand chain", which would start with the users rather than investment and would have the following characteristics:

- End Users, who would be empowered to procure the physical and virtual environments they need to accommodate their work and their social, intellectual and cultural lives from a wide variety of sources and suppliers. Demand would be measured not by long-term commitments to pay so many dollars per square foot peryear or euros per square metre per month but by how much users are willing to pay by the day and even by the hour for the spaces and services that meet their requirements. We have, after all, long been accustomed to procure space and services in hotels from a wide variety of competitive sources in exactly this way;

- Corporate Real Estate and Facilities Managers and other suppliers who would be principally rewarded, like the best restaurateurs and hoteliers, for the degree to which they satisfy their customers as well as for the skill with which they deliver and maintain highly sustainable environments;

- Design and Construction professionals and firms from the Architect via the Planners to the Cost Consultants, various kinds of Engineer, Project Managers, Construction Managers, Sub-contractors and Suppliers who were principally concerned with and rewarded for making the most imaginative and efficient use—and above all—reuse of existing accommodation at every scale from the cafe table to the city. This enlightened and responsive delivery process would take account oh the utility of all office space and only occasionally would find it necessary to invest in new construction;

- Finance and Development providers: from Investors to Developers to Lawyers, Letting Agents and Real Estate Brokers—who would profit less from always moving on to new projects and new construction but more from intelligently and sustainably managing what exists already on the model of the best practice of the great London estates such as Grosvenor and Howard de Walden.[26]

26 Groak, Steven, *Is Construction an Industry?*, Construction Management and Economics, 1994, p. 12

Just to add an ironic, early twenty-first century twist, these words were written in a brand new hotel room in Burj Dubai looking out at mile after mile of perhaps the most mindless construction the world has ever seen—the product of the wrong supply chain operating in the wrong way for the wrong reasons.

The reversal of the wasteful and destructive Taylorist supply chain in order to create a demand-led system of delivery is the first necessary

The Networked Office

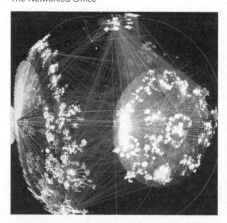
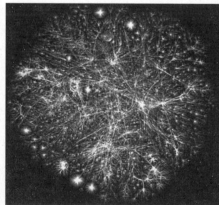

NON-CORE SPACE
Managed by others

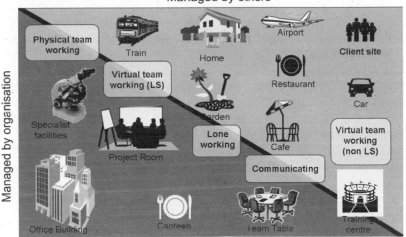

CORE SPACE
Managed by organisation

Physical team working

Train

Home

Airport

Client site

Specialist facilities

Virtual team working (LS)

Garden

Restaurant

Car

Lone working

Cafe

Virtual team working (non LS)

Project Room

Communicating

Office Building

Canteen

Team Table

Training centre

Allocating space on the basis of work pattern

condition for creating the environment of the knowledge economy, which I shall call "The Networked Office". Networked Offices are the appropriate response to the demands of our increasingly mobile knowledge economy because they will combine the potential of virtuality and the power of physicality. Networked Offices will transcend conventional architectural boundaries to take advantage of entirely different kinds of relationship between technology and people and between time and place. The three major advantages of Networked Offices are that they would provide the potential; firstly, of making knowledge based work more enjoyable and compatible with other activities, secondly, of facilitating more efficient and effective use of existing buildings and cities and, thirdly, and most importantly is the context of this argument of making a huge contribution to creating sustainable cities. The challenge of designing Networked Offices to satisfy intelligent and demanding knowledge workers will also have the effect of weaning architects from our obsession with new building towards making the most imaginative and creative use of what already exists.

JUSTIFYING PLACE IN AN INCREASINGLY VIRTUAL WORLD

I have taken part recently in two tele-presence conferences. The first was at Cisco's offices near Heathrow. Only two of those taking part were in London, the other participants were in San Francisco. The second was a workshop at Hewlett Packard's offices in the City of London, linking attendees from Boston, Palo Alto and London.

My experience in both conferences of sharing a meeting table, half of which is real and half virtual, was not unlike being on the other side of the table in Leonardo da Vinci's *Last Supper*. But so perfect are the life size images of the virtual participants, so clear is every feature, nuance of expression, flicker of the eye lids, and so precisely synchronised are vision and sound, that within two or three minutes all disbelief is suspended.

A Cisco
Telepresence
Room

At the end of my second tele-presence experience, I had become
so absorbed in what had been a very successful workshop
discussion that I forgot where I was. When the session was over
and the participants were dispersing, we had been unplugged
for sound but the vision remained on the screens. I could see Bill
Porter, my old friend and colleague from MIT leaving the Boston
part of the meeting. I had a personal question to ask him and I
found myself going up to his image on the screen to attract his
attention. He saw me, turned with a surprised glance towards me
but, of course, couldn't hear me. Like Hamlet's father's ghost, he
turned away: I was talking and gesticulating to a shade. Such was
the physical impact on me of a powerful virtual experience.

How best to explore the potential impact of information
technology on work, workplaces and the wider environment?
Let me suggest a mental experiment. Imagine an entirely virtual
world populated by virtual beings who enjoy all the power and
convenience of virtuality. One day a virtual genius within this
virtual paradise lights upon the notion of physical place. What
arguments would this virtual being, a new Lucifer, have to muster
to transcend the limiting conventions of virtuality? What evidence
would this being have to assemble to persuade his or her fellows

that real places, physical spaces, with all their lumpiness, stiffness, messiness and cost are capable of complementing and enhancing the benefits of virtuality?

A null hypothesis, at least as vivid and sweeping as the one sketched above, is needed to challenge inherited assumptions about the nature of time and place. Temporal and spatial conventions do not invent themselves. Like the supply chains discussed above, they are also cultural constructs for which we must take responsibility. Architects in particular in this rapidly changing world need to be challenged out of our complacency. We must justify our contribution to society, indeed our very existence. Safer to start again from nothing, to go back to first principles, to invent workplaces and ways of using cities that are appropriate to the emerging technology and economy of the twenty-first century. To rethink the workplace and ultimately the city it is necessary is to take all existing design prescriptions, typologies and formulae with a very large pinch of salt.

The value of place—what long ago was called *genuis loci*—continues to be enormous but we architects must realise that the monopoly of place on how we construct reality is being strongly challenged by the burgeoning power and convenience of virtuality. Several arguments justifying the value of place come to mind.

Firstly; places are impregnated with memory, association, recall and resonance.

Secondly; places are excellent at opening up unanticipated opportunities—they engender, as I mentioned earlier, "serendipity"—the happy coincidences that cities make more probable, that occur at parties and social events, the kind of opportunity from which I was prematurely unplugged at my tele-presence séance described above.

Chance is embedded in streets, in non-linear events, in surprise, in open-endedness, in the coincidences that belong to a non-programmed world. As Pasteur said about research, "chance favours the prepared mind".

Thirdly; place promotes sociability and networking. Conversely place always offers the potential to withdraw, to remove oneself discreetly when necessary.

Fourthly; place is good at expressing meaning: subtlety, beauty, pleasure—the qualities that Lewis Mumford described as "the culture of cities".[27]

27 Mumford, Lewis, The Culture of Cities, New York: Secker & Warburg, 1938

Finally; place, at its best, both registers and controls degrees of intimacy in human interaction. Nolli's famous map of eighteenth century Rome needs to be redrawn in terms of a newly relevant's typology of permeable, semi-permeable and private spaces. Even within the binary convention of Nolli's figure-ground drawing, you see just at a glance that the Piazza Navona, the Pantheon, the churches, the monasteries, markets, courtyards, streets aggregate to about 30 per cent of the ground area. The drawing reveals a highly permeable urban structure that is very far from the genius for exclusion that is one of the sadder characteristics of the twentieth century city.

Richard Sennett criticises brittle buildings that can only accommodate one function. Stewart Brand advocates buildings that can learn, that have the capacity to accommodate growth and change, that get better rather than deteriorate over time. Both cities and buildings should also offer, not just two or even three, but many degrees of permeability which can be managed to foster cultural and intellectual discourse. In the knowledge economy we will measure places, both buildings and cities, by the amount of knowledge that is accumulated and quantity of ideas that are generated within their fabric.

THE CRISIS

In the knowledge economy more and more businesses, both large and small, will operate as networks, depending at least as much on virtual communications as on face to face interactions. Networked organisations do not need to operate, manage or define themselves within conventional categories of workplaces or conventional working hours.

- Office buildings in their present state are neither a stable nor a sustainable building type;

- Much office space today is already under-occupied and under-used. Unless patterns of occupancy are radically changed, offices are certain to become even less densely occupied as confidence in distributed working increases;

- Much conventional office space, especially top quality, Grade A space, is likely to be unsuitable for emerging ways of working and will be difficult to convert to emerging business uses and even more difficult to convert to alternative uses;

- Conventional office developments exclude or marginalise workspace at lower rental levels and thus diminish the possibility of mutually beneficial interactions between large, mature businesses and smaller, growing enterprises;

- Conventional office developments sterilise opportunities for the growth of embryonic businesses;

- Conventional office developments do not provide enough interstitial space to accommodate inter-company transactions, mobile workers or the overlapping activities that are characteristic of networked working.

Putting these arguments into the context of the wider debate about sustainability and climate change leads to the conclusion that the issue is not simply the technical specification of energy use and carbon emissions of new office buildings (already only a fraction of the problem) but wider issues of general over supply, large-scale under use and poor facilities management. Office buildings occupied by conventional businesses are already contributing massively to the degradation of the planet. In relation to the emerging needs of networked twenty-first century businesses the total environmental performance of offices is likely to deteriorate further and faster.

Let us put the argument even more strongly: the Taylorist office building has been a perfect machine for delivering environmental degradation because it is so completely the product of supply side thinking which overrides user interests, ignores the public good and takes no account of collateral damage. The corollary of this statement is that to save the planet it will not be enough for architects—accepting for the sake of argument an entirely illogical and contradictory proposition—to design an improved, more environmentally sustainable version of the Taylorist office. I made an analogous mistake two decades ago when I thought that the emerging profession of what I hope would be user-facing Facilities Managers would lead to more responsible office design. What happened was simply that Facilities Management itself became almost instantly part of the supply chain, largely preferring pain free delivery to the hard work of helping users decide what needs to be delivered.

A more radical approach is necessary to arrest the waste; abandoning the Taylorist supply chain completely. Replacing the Taylorist supply chain with the Social Democratic model would be better but almost certainly not enough given the contradictions inherent in that generous but somewhat self indulgent and introspective process. However, the Networked Office, because it embraces the entirely different use of space and time made possible by Information Technology, currently has the potential for effecting real and substantial change for the better. The reconfiguration of the workplace combined with radical rethinking of the pattern of use of working and living spaces over time supported by the introduction of a user based and responsible, demand-led system of procurement and delivery are the three necessary components of the complete answer.

We are lucky to be living in a time when these possibilities exist. We are unlucky to live in a time when they are so urgently necessary.

THE SUSTAINABLE CITY

Some have argued that powerful, reliable and above all ubiquitous Information Technology will encourage universal suburbanisation on the Californian model—endless tracts of comfortable, electronically enhanced, individual McMansions interrupted only by the occasional freeway.

My vision of the future city is almost exactly the opposite. It is essentially urban. The vision depends upon the social logic of the knowledge economy which will thrive on open ended discourse much of which will be aided by technology but that will also continue to be social, plural and face to face.

The vision is equally dependant upon the economic logic of sustainability which will discourage excessive reliance on the car and air travel and, equally important, will encourage much more intensive use of existing spatial resources.

The development of the knowledge economy and achievement of sustainability will both be made possible by the power of Information Technology. All three factors operating together will create the conditions for a renaissance of the city.

The sustainable city will have to be very different from most existing cities and certainly from those cities that have been most violently shaped by the Modern Movement in architecture and by the Taylorist ideas of division and exclusion that underpinned that movement. To reverse Richard Sennett's critique of the twentieth century city the sustainable city must be designed to make possible:

- closer adjacencies between buildings of different scales, e.g. making sure that appropriate scale buildings and spaces for smaller tenants can be accommodated very close to or even above, under or within larger structures suitable for larger and medium size tenants;

- multi functionality through the planned juxtaposition of complementary and mutually supportive uses within a varied regime of rental levels and forms of tenure. An example of this is the growing need for short term, relatively cheap accommodation suitable for smaller creative businesses within fashion, media and design, e.g. rough and ready, short-term loft spaces, in which concepts can be conceived, developed and produced which are closely adjacent to the larger, more stable businesses that can deliver but which need instant and ongoing access to the most fickle and transient environment of creativity;

- the provision and maintenance of a very large amount
  and a wide range of attractive interstitial places and
  spaces, permeable in various degrees, designed to
  make possible the maximum number of serendipitous
  encounters between businesses and enterprises of many
  different kinds, sizes, highly networked individuals as well
  as between cultures and levels of resource.

The requirements of the sustainable city will contradict a great
deal of obsolete twentieth century planning legislation—mixing
uses, overlapping sectors, bringing together activities and
social groups that have long been artificially kept apart.
Densities of occupation in conventional terms will have to be
as high as are the densest parts of Manhattan and Hong Kong
today. More importantly patterns of use over time, 24 hours a
day, seven days a week, will have to be far more intense than
any experienced today, even in the most lively quarters of the
most vital existing cities.

Expect the intermeshing of building uses and types, especially
the obsolescent office building, and a vast improvement of the
capacity of all buildings and all spaces between buildings to
accommodate change and improvement over time. Anticipate
the organisational protocols and the physical accommodation
that will provide the many degrees of permeability (and
security) that will be required in a highly interactive knowledge-
based economy. Look forward to cities where calm, quiet
and rest are generously provided in residences, gardens and
parks; contrasting with and complementing the social realm.
It will be impossible to tell where universities, libraries and
other academic and intellectual institutions begin and where
they end, since a high proportion of the building stock will be
given over to collective spaces designed to accommodate
intellectual and social discourse. Vertical circulation will
be designed to be generous and visible. Expect a higher
proportion of the city's space to be given over to horizontal
public access and circulation—streets, squares and plazas

enlivened by busy frontages and, like Bryant Square in New York, enhanced by universal access to the ever-present internet. Despite their shifting boundaries, the virtual and the physical realms will support and complement each other.

The renaissance of the city is, of course, highly desirable. The three conditions under which it is likely to happen already exist— the growing importance of the knowledge economy, the urgent threat of climate change, the ready availability and increasing power of Information Technology. The one other factor that will be necessary to achieve this vision is to reverse the dismal, dominant, suboptimal, feedback free, development driven supply chain that has caused so much trouble, generated so much waste and grievously distorted much urban development throughout the very unsatisfactory twentieth century.

Trust the users, abandon supply-side thinking, prioritise sustainability, take advantage of technology and we will have a fighting chance of getting cities we can enjoy, of building the knowledge-based culture our economy needs and, let's hope, of saving the planet at the same time.

SUGGESTED READING

General

"Barker Review of Land Use Planning", Department of Communities and Local Government, 2006.

Florida, Richard, The Rise of the Creative Class, London: Basic Books, 2002.

Foxell Simon, ed., The professionals' choice: The future of the built environment professions, London: Building Futures, 2003.

Kunstler, James Howard, The Long Emergency, Atlantic Monthly Press, 2005.

Leadbeater, Charles, Personalisation through participation: A new script for public services, London: Demos, 2004.

Schumacher, EF, Small is Beautiful, Vancouver: Hartley & Marks,1999.

Economic Survey of the United Kingdom, OECD, 2007.
World Population Prospects: The 2006 Revision, Population Division of the Department of Economic and Social Affairs of the United Nations Secretariat, United Nations, 2007.

Planet Earth and Climate Change

Flannery, Tim, The Weather Makers: The History and Future Impact of Climate Change, Melbourne: Text Publishing, 2005.

Gore, Al, Earth in the Balance: Ecology and the Human Spirit, Boston: Houghton Mifflin, 1992.

Gore, Al, The Assault on Reason, Harmondsworth: Penguin, 2007.

Hartmann, Thom, Last Hours of Ancient Sunlight, New York: Three Rivers Press, 1997 (rev. 2004).

Hawken, Lovins & Lovins, Natural Capitalism, London: Little Brown, 1999.

Hillman, Mayer, How We Can Save the Planet, Harmondsworth: Penguin, 2004.

Homer-Dixon, Thomas, The Upside of Down: Catastrophe, Creativity and the Renewal of Civilisation, New York: Alfred A Knopf, 2006.

Kolbert, Elizabeth, Field Notes from a Catastrophe: A Frontline Report on Climate Change, London: Bloomsbury, 2006.

Lovelock, James, Gaia: A New Look at Life on Earth, Oxford: Oxford University Press, 1979.

Lovelock, James, The Revenge of Gaia, London: Allen Lane, 2006.

Lynas, Mark, High Tide: The Truth About Our Climate Crisis, London: Picador, 2004.

Lynas, Mark, Six Degrees: Our Future on a Hotter Planet, London: Fourth Estate, 2007.

Marshall, George, Carbon Detox, London: Gaia Thinking, 2007.

McDonough, W, and Braungert M, Cradle to Cradle, Remaking the Way We Make Things, New York: North Point Press, 2002.

Monbiot, George, *Heat: How We Can Stop the Planet Burning*, London: Allen Lane, 2006.

Walker, G, and King D, *The Hot Topic: How to Tackle Global Warming and Still Keep the Lights On*, London: Bloomsbury, 2008.

Action Today to Protect Tomorrow—The Mayor's Climate Change Action Plan, London: GLA, 2007.

Climate Change The UK Programme, London: DEFRA, 2006.

Summary for Policymakers of the Synthesis Report of the IPCC Fourth Assessment Report, United Nations, 2007.

Cities

Girardet, Herbert, *Cities People Planet: Liveable Cities for a Sustainable World*, Chichester: Wiley-Academy, 2004.

Jacobs, Jane, *The Death and Life of Great American Cities*, New York: Random House, 1961.

Jacobs, Jane, *The Economy of Cities*, New York: Random House, 1969.

Mumford, Lewis, *The Culture of Cities*, New York: Secker & Warburg, 1938.

Sudjic, Deyan, "Cities on the edge of chaos", *The Observer*, March 2008.

Urban Task Force, *Towards an Urban Renaissance*, London: E&FN Spon, 1999.

Work

Abramson, Daniel M, *Building the Bank of England*, New Haven, CT: Yale University Press, 2005.

Alexander, Christopher, *The Timeless Way of Building*, Oxford: Oxford University Press, 1979.

Anderson, Ray, *Mid-Course Correction: The Interface Model*, Chelsea Green, 2007.

Brand, Stewart, *How Buildings Learn*, New York: Viking Press, 1994.

Brinkley, Ian, *Defining the Knowledge Economy, Knowledge Economy Programme Report*, London: The Work Foundation, 2006.

Castells, Manuel, *The Information Age: Economy, Society, Culture*, Oxford: Blackwell, 1996.

Davenport, Tom, *Thinking for a Living*, Boston: Harvard Business School Press, 2005.

Dodgson, Gann, and Salter, *Think, Play, Do*, Oxford, 2005.

Dodgson, Gann and Salter, *The management of technological innovation strategy and practice*, Oxford: Oxford University Press, 2008.

Duffy, Francis, *The Changing Workplace*, London: Phaidon, 1992.

Duffy, Francis, *The New Office*, London: Conran Octopus, 1997.

Duffy, Francis, *Architectural Knowledge*, London: E&FN Spon, 1998.

Duffy, Cave, Worthington, *Planning Office Space*, London: The Architectural Press, 1976.

Galloway, L, *Office Management: Its Principles and Practice*, Oxford: The Ronald Press, 1918.

Gann, David, *Building Innovation*, London: Thomas Telford, 2000.

Giedion, Siegfried, *Mechanization Takes Command*, Oxford: Oxford University Press, 1948.

Gilbreth, FB, *Motion Study*, New York: Van Nostrand, 1911.

Gottfried, David, *Greed to Green*, Berkeley, CA: Worldbuild Publishing, 2004.

Groak, Steven, *Is Construction an Industry?*, Construction Management and Economics, 1994.

Handy, Charles, *Understanding Organizations*, Harmondsworth: Penguin, 1967.

Hawken, Paul, *The Ecology of Commerce*, New York: HarperCollins, 1993.

Mitchell, William J, *City of Bits*, Cambridge, MA: MIT Press, 1995.

Quinan, Jack, *Frank Lloyd Wright's Larkin Building*, Cambridge, MA: MIT Press, 1987.

Sassen, Saskia, *A Sociology of Globalization*, New York: Norton, 2006.

Sennett, Richard, *The Culture of the New Capitalism*, New Haven, CT: Yale University Press, 2006.

Taylor, Frederick, *The Principles of Scientific Management*, New York: Harper & Brothers, 1911.

Trease, Geoffrey, *Samuel Pepys and His World*, London: Thames and Hudson, 1972.

Education

Aston and Bekhradnia, *Demand for Graduates: A review of the economic evidence*, Higher Education Policy Institute, 2003.

Friere, Paolo, *Education: the practice of freedom*, London: Writers and Readers Cooperative, 1974.

Gardner, Howard, *Multiple Intelligences*, New York: Basic Books, 1993.

Goodman, Paul, *Growing up absurd*, New York: First Sphere Books, 1970.

Illich, Ivan, *Deschooling Society*, London: Calder and Boyars.1971.

Kimber, Mike, Does Size Matter? *Distributed leadership in small secondary schools*, National College for School Leadership, 2003.

Nair and Fielding, *The Language of School Design*, DesignShare, 2005.

Neil, AS, Summerhill, Harmondsworth: Penguin Books,1968. *The Children's Plan—Building Brighter Futures*, DCSF, December 2007.

Every Child Matters: Change for Children, DfES/ HM Government, 2004.

Higher Standards, Better Schools For All, DfES.

2020 Vision Report of the Teaching and Learning in 2020, Review Group, 2006.

www.smallschools.org.uk

www.thecademy.net/ inclusiontrust.org/ Welcome.html

www.eco-schools.org.uk

www.standards.dfes.gov.uk/ personalisedlearning/about/

Transport and Neighbourhoods

Banister, David, *Unsustainable Transport: City Transport in the New Century*, London: E&FN Spon, 2005.

Bertolini L, and T, Spit, *Cities on Rails. The Redevelopment of Railway Station Areas*, London: Spon/Routledge, 1998.

Calthorpe P, and Fulton, W, *The Regional City: Planning for the End of Sprawl*, Washington, DC: Island Press, 2003.

Dittmar H, and Ohland, G, *The New Transit Town: Best Practices in Transit-Oriented Development*, Washington, DC: Island Press, 2004.

Hickman, R and Banister, D, *Looking over the horizon, Transport and reduced CO_2 emissions in the UK by 2030*, Transport Policy, 2007.

Holtzclaw, Clear, Dittmar, Goldstein and Haas, *Location Efficiency: Neighborhood and Socioeconomic Characteristics Determine Auto Ownership and Use*, Transportation Planning and Technology (Vol. 25) 2002.

Commission for Integrated Transport, Planning for High Speed Rail Needed Now, 2004, viewed at http://www.cfit.gov.uk/pn/040209/index.htm

Regional Transport Statistics, National Statistics and Department for Transport, 2006 Edition.

Energy, Transport and Environment Indicators, Eurostat, 2005 Edition.

Toward a Sustainable Transport system, Department for Transport, 2007.

Eddington Transport Study, HM Treasury & Department for Transport, 2007.

UK Foresight programme, *Tackling Obesities: Future Choices*, The Government Office for Science and Technology, 2007.

Community

Dench G, Gavron K, and Young M, *The New East End: Kinship*, Race and Conflict, London: Profile, 2006.

Jacobs, Jane, *The Death and Life of American Cities*, New York: Modern Library, 1961.

Putnam, Robert, *Bowling Alone: The Collapse and Revival of American Community*, New York: Simon & Schuster, 2000.

Young M, and Willmott, P, *Family and Kinship in East London*, Harmondsworth: Penguin, 1957.

Report Card 7, *Child poverty in perspective: An overview of child well-being in rich countries*, UNICEF Innocenti Research Centre, 2007.

Key Facts for Diverse Communities: Ethnicity and Faith, Greater London Authority, Data Management and Analysis Group, 2007.

www.footprintnetwork.org

www.yourhistoryhere

www.fixmystreet.com

Globalisation

Abbott, C, Rogers, P, Sloboda, J, *Global Responses to Global Threats: Sustainable Security for the 21st Century*, Oxford: The Oxford Research Group, 2006.

Balls E, Healey J and Leslie C, *Evolution and Devolution in England*, New Local Government Network, 2006.

Gladwell, Malcolm, *The Tipping Point: How Little Things Can Make a Big Difference*, London: Little Brown, 2000.

Goldsmith, Edward, "How to Feed People under a Regime of Climate Change", *Ecologist Magazine*, 2004.

Gore, Al, *The Assault on Reason*, London: Bloomsbury, 2007.

Gray, John, *Black Mass: Apocalyptic Religion and the Death of Utopia*, London: Allen Lane, 2007.

Guillebaud, John, *Youthquake: Population, Fertility and Environment in the 21st Century*, Optimum Population Trust, 2007.

Hines, Colin, *Localisation: A Global Manifesto*, London: Earthscan, 2000.

Kagan, Robert, *Of Paradise and Power: America and Europe in the New World Order*, New York: Alfred Knopf, 2003.

Martin, James, *The Meaning of the 21st Century*, London: Transworld, 2007.

Meadows, Meadows, Randers and Behrens, *Limits to Growth*, Club of Rome, 1972.

Nordhaus, T, and M, Shellenberger, *Break Through: From the Death of Environmentalism to the Politics of Possibility*, Boston: Houghton Mifflin, 2007.

Porritt, Jonathon, *Capitalism: As if the World Matters*, London: Earthscan, 2005.

Roszak, Theodore, *World Beware! American Triumphalism in an Age of Terror*, Toronto: Between the Lines, 2006.

Sachs, W, and T, Santarius *Fair Future: Resource Conflicts, Security and Global Justice*, London: Zed Books, 2005.

Kirkpatrick Sale, *Dwellers in the Land*, New Society Publishers, 1991.

Shrybman, Steven, *A Citizen's Guide to the World Trade Organisation*, Ottawa, Canadian Center for Policy Alternatives, 1999.

Soros, George, *The Age of Fallability: The Consequences of the War on Terror*, Beverly Hills, CA: Phoenix Books, 2006.

Stern, Nicholas, *The Economics of Climate Change: The Stern Review*, Cambridge: Cambridge University Press, 2007.

Stiglitz, Joseph, *Globalization and its Discontents*, New York: Norton, 2002.

Stiglitz, Joseph, *Making Globalization Work*, New York: Norton, 2006.

Wolf, Martin, *Why Globalization Works*, New Haven, CT: Yale University Press, 2005.

Johannesburg Manifesto, Fairness in a Fragile World, Berlin: Heinrich Böll Foundation, 2002

US Defence Dept, *An Abrupt Climate Change Scenario and It's Implications for US Natural Security*, 2003.

WWF, Living Planet Report, WWI International, 2006.

Further websites

The Edge
www.at-the-edge.org.uk

CABE
www.cabe.org.uk

China Dialogue
www.chinadialogue.net

Global Commons Institute (Contraction and Convergence)
www.gci.org.uk

AUTHORS

David Gann

David Gann is Professor of Innovation and Technology Management at Imperial College London and Group Innovation Executive, Laing O'Rourke. His personal research includes work recently published in *Think, Play Do: Technology, Innovation and Organization*, co-authored with Mark Dodgson and Ammon Salter, on the intensification of innovation.

Frank Duffy

Frank Duffy CBE is a founder of the international multi-disciplinary consultancy practice, DEGW. He was Visiting Professor at MIT 2001–2004, President of the RIBA 1993–1995 and is a founding member of the Edge. He has written and edited several books, including *The New Office*, 1997, and *Architectural Knowledge*, 1998.

ACKNOWLEDGEMENT

This paper could not have been written without the extensive body of thought, research and design related to the changing nature of work and the working environment that my colleagues in DEGW have built up collaboratively over the years—a body of work for which I am deeply grateful.

Frank Duffy

THE EDGE

The Edge is a ginger group and think tank, sponsored by the building industry professions, that seeks to stimulate public interest in policy questions that affect the built environment, and to inform and influence public opinion. It was established in 1996 with support from the Arup Foundation. The Edge is supported by The Carbon Trust.

The Edge organises a regular series of debates and other events intended to advance policy thinking in the built environment sector and among the professional bodies within it. For further details, see www.at-the-edge.org.uk

EDGE FUTURES

Edge Futures is a project initiated by The Edge and Black Dog Publishing. It has only been possible with the active participation of The Edge Committee as well as supporting firms and institutions. Special thanks are due to Adam Poole, Duncan McCorquodale, Frank Duffy, Robin Nicholson, Bill Gething, Chris Twinn, Andy Ford, Mike Murray and Jane Powell as well as to all the individual authors.

The project has been generously sponsored by The Carbon Trust, The Commission for Architecture and the Built Environment (CABE), Ramboll Whitbybird, The Arup Foundation, ProLogis and Construction Skills. Thanks are due to all those bodies and to the support of Karen Germain, Elanor Warwick, Mark Whitby, Ken Hall and Guy Hazlehurst within them. The Edge is also grateful to Sebastian Macmillan of IDBE in Cambridge for the day we spent developing scenarios there and to Philip Guildford for facilitating the session.

Simon Foxell

Much is already known about the state of the world
15 to 20 years from now. Almost all the buildings and
infrastructure are already in place or in development—we
replace our buildings etc., at a very slow pace. The great
majority of the population who'll be living and working
then, especially in the UK, have already been born and
will have been educated in a school system that is familiar
and predictable. The global population, however, will have
increased from 6.7 billion in July 2007 to approximately 8
billion by 2025.

The climate will have changed, mainly as a result of the
emissions of greenhouse gases of the past 50 and more
years, but not by much. The temperature is predicted to be,
on average, half a degree warmer, as well as varying over a
greater range than at present. But, more significantly it will be
understood to be changing, resulting in a strong feeling of
uncertainty and insecurity. Rainfall will have reduced but will
also become more extreme, i.e. tending to drought or flood.
Resources, whether energy, water or food imports, will be in
shorter supply; partly as a result of climate change but also
due to regulations aimed at preventing the effects of global
warming becoming worse. Transport will be constrained as a
result but other technologies will have greatly improved the
ability to economically communicate.

These changes form the context for this first series of five
Edge Futures books, but it is not their subject: that is the
impact of such changes and other developments on our
daily lives, the economy, social and education services
and the way the world trades and operates. Decision
makers are already being challenged to act and formulate
policy, in the face of the change already apparent in the
years ahead. This set of books highlights how critical and
important planning for the future is going to be. Society
will expect and require policy makers to have thought
ahead and prepared for the best as well as the worst. Edge

Futures offers a series of critical views of events, in the next two decades, that need to be planned for today.

The five books intentionally look at the future from very different viewpoints and perspectives. Each author, or pair of authors, has been asked to address a different sector of society, but there is inevitably a great deal of crossover between them. They do not always agree; but consistency is not the intention; that is to capture a breadth of vision as where we may be in 20 years time.

Jonathon Porritt in *Globalism and Regionalism* examines some of the greatest challenges before the planet, including climate change and demographic growth, and lays down the gauntlet to the authors of the other books. Porritt's diagnosis of the need to establish a new balance between the global and the regional over the years ahead and to achieve a 'Civic Globalisation' has an echo in Geoff Mulgan's call in *Living and Community* for strengthening communities through rethinking local governance and rebuilding a sense of place. Both are—perhaps professionally—optimistic that the climate change is a challenge that we, as a society, can deal with, while not underestimating the change that our society is going to have to undergo to achieve it.

Hank Dittmar, writing in *Transport and Networks* is less than certain, that currently, policies are adequately joined-up to deal with the issues that the recent flurry of major reports from the UK Government has highlighted: "Planning" from Barker, "Climate Change" from Stern and "Transport" from Eddington. He notes Barker's comment that "planning plays a role in the mitigation of and adaptation to climate change, the biggest issue faced across all climate areas"but that she then goes on to dismiss the issue. In its approach to all these reviews, the government has shown that it is more concerned with economic growth and indeed it has already concluded that the transport network needs no further fundamental reform. Dittmar believes otherwise, he calls for immediate solutions to support the development of the accessible, sustainable city.

Simon Foxell in *Education and Creativity* sees an even bumpier ride ahead, with progress only being made as a result of the lurch from crisis to crisis. Such discontinuities, will allow the UK to address many longstanding problems, from the personalisation of education to addressing the increasingly cut-throat international competition in creativity, innovation and skills—but not without a great deal of pain and chaos. Bill Mitchell, in the same volume, outlines a way of reconfiguring educational practice to develop just those skills that successful creativity-based economies are going to require.

In *Working*, Frank Duffy sees the end of road for the classic 'American Taylorist' office and the unsuitability of its counterpart, the European social democratic office. In their place, he proposes a new typology—the networked office—that will make better use of the precious resource that is our existing stock of buildings and allow greater integration into the life of the city. And, it is the city that all the authors come back to as a central and unifying theme—the dominant form of the millennium, the place where the majority of mankind now lives. Perhaps this is because, as Deyan Sudjic, Director of the Design Museum, has written recently; "The future of the city has suddenly become the only subject in town."

It is about the largest social unit that most of us can imagine with any ease and is a constant challenge economically, socially and environmentally. If we can work out what a sustainable city might be like and how to deliver it, then maybe we can sleep easier in our beds, less afraid that the end of civilisation, as we recognise it, may be within our childrens', or our childrens' childrens', lifetime. All the component parts of the Edge Futures studies come together in the city; where the community meets the office buildings, the schools and transport system. The city is the hub of the regional response to world events and needs to become a responsive participant in formulating a way out of policy log-jam.

As this first series of Edge Futures shows, the task is urgent and deeply complex but also not impossible. It is only, assuming that we need to make the transition to a low carbon economy within ten to twenty years, in Geoff Mulgan's words: "extraordinarily challenging by any historic precedent."

10a Acton Street
London WC1X 9NG
T. +44 (0)20 7613 1922
F. +44 (0)20 7613 1944
E. info@blackdogonline.com
W. www.blackdogonline.com

Designed by Draught Associates

All opinions expressed within this publication are those of the authors and
not necessarily of the publisher.

British Library Cataloguing-in-Publication Data.
A CIP record for this book is available from the British Library.
ISBN: 978 1 906155 124

Black Dog Publishing, London, UK is an environmentally responsible
company. Edge Futures are printed on Cyclus Offset, a paper produced
from 100% post consumer waste.

architecture art design
fashion history photography
theory and things

black dog
publishing

www.blackdogonline.com

4377 313